A FATHER'S HEART

Rosary Meditations for Dads

Doug Lorig

Caritas Press, USA

A FATHER'S HEART
Rosary Meditations for Dads

Doug Lorig

For information regarding permission, contact Sherry@LilyTrilogy.com

First Edition

10 9 8 7 6 5 4 3 2 1

ISBN 978-0-9833866-5-0

For reorders, visit LilyTrilogy.com or CatholicWord.com

Published by Caritas Press, Arizona, USA

INTRODUCTION

The demands on our time seem endless. Little League games, school plays, birthday parties. Yard work, fix-it lists and trips to the hardware store. Middle-of-the-night bellyaches, monsters under the bed and bouts of teething. And, of course, there's work. Deadlines and quotas and traffic jams. Why should busy fathers take time to pray the rosary?

Simply put, we can't hope to accomplish all the things we are called to do as fathers if we are not in touch with the Divine. We need the Holy Spirit. He is our guide, our light, our strength and our sanity. Apart from Him, we can do nothing. With His help, there is no limit to the love we can build within our families.

When we pray the Holy Rosary, meditating on the life, death and resurrection of Jesus, the Holy Spirit comes to us in a powerful way, infusing His ways into our ways. As Mary's spouse, He lovingly and joyfully guides us as we ask our Blessed Mother's intercession to help us fulfill our call to holiness.

May these meditations give you a growing gratitude for the gift of fatherhood and lead you ever closer to the heart of God.

THE JOYFUL MYSTERIES

I

THE ANNUNCIATION

"May it be done to me." *Luke 1:38*

I remember standing beside my wife as she gave birth to our first child. It was a powerful spiritual moment. All we had wanted was to get the birthing behind us and hold this new life we had "created" nine months earlier. When he finally appeared, I cried. My wife, on the other hand, was very busy, and didn't cry until later. What I did not think of at the time, but have reflected on deeply these days, is that not only did our genetic packages define a great deal for this boy, but God's "genetic contribution" defines him in an even more wonderful way. Our Father in heaven gave my son God's own image! At the moment of conception, God bestowed on him the gift of a rational soul with the powers to reason, to will, to imagine and to create an endless variety of beauty. He gave the supreme gift: the gift of life – a life that goes on forever. My wife and I are co-creators with God, contributing to the existence of an eternal being, designed out of love for love. How amazing is that!

With all the day-to-day parenting needed to raise our kids, we rarely think to put the healing of God's image in them at the top of our list. Children enter the world sweet and innocent. We don't think of these precious bundles as "sinners." But in a couple of years, we will hear their "no!" and "mine!" and witness the start of their own free-fall in-to the passions of our fallen nature.

As I pray this First Joyful Mystery, may God help me to rejoice again in the creation of my children. And may He give me the grace and love to model holiness, beauty and our Catholic teachings, that these may become gifts my children desire with the burning of their hearts, and not something I force on them. Holy Spirit, I entrust my fatherhood to you!

II

THE VISITATION

"At the moment the sound of your greeting reached my ears, the infant in my womb leaped for joy."

Luke 1:44

While she held the savior of the world within her womb, Mary went to visit and help her relative Elizabeth, who, at an old age, was expecting her first child. The Holy Spirit used this family event to introduce the two infants in their mothers' wombs and to write a wonderful theology that would proclaim the blessedness of the unborn.

But the event teaches us something else too. Mary lovingly made the journey to Elizabeth's house because it was a family obligation. The visitation was an event based on love and the obligations attached to that love. As I pray this mystery, I need to realize that, as Blessed John Paul II tells us, God made the family a school of love, reflective of God Himself, who is a family of persons - Father, Son, and Holy Spirit. I want to instill in my children this value of family, modeled after what Jesus has revealed about the love to be nurtured in that environment.

Love of God and love of neighbor hold first place in the Wisdom of the Spirit. In the family, that means the gift of self. I remember how this truth came home to me when we were teaching our kids to share. Sharing is all about parting, out of love, with what is "mine." Sharing because we are threatened is not love at all, but fear - a product of coercion, not a gift to the beloved. Sharing out of love is what my children did naturally when they offered me a bite of their soggy teething biscuit - with much love written all over their little faces.

As my children grow away from the generosity of early childhood, may I be an example for them of love in action - of a love that is more than a nice philosophy, but a gift of my very self. Holy Spirit, I entrust my fatherhood to You.

III

THE NATIVITY

"You will find an infant wrapped in swaddling clothes and lying in a manger."
Luke 2:12

All Christians and many non-Christians would agree that the birth of Jesus in Bethlehem is an event of cosmic proportions. His meaning for us, as well as his impact on the whole of mankind, make Christmas a celebration that even the secular culture promotes on some level. For me, the birth of each of my own children was an event of cosmic proportions - not only because of the "mine" involved in their coming, but also because they are children of God and creatures endowed with the image of God Himself! In this truth, I see every pregnancy as supremely beautiful: planned, unwanted, producing a deformed fetus - they are all equally sublime. Every pregnancy is an event of cosmic proportions because of God's image hidden within it and because every person is precious to God.

Intellectual arguments against abortion are valuable. Those full of theology are even better. We have to remember, though, when our children step into the higher grades and onto the college campus, someone will have a "better" argument in favor of abortion. But no one can argue with authentic love. I want my children to be formed by my love. I want them to see through that love, to the love of the Creator, who loves without measure everything He creates. I want them to see, through His eyes, the dignity of the human fetus - noble, endowed by God with His very image, and gifted with the potential of living with Him forever. I want my children to know that God loves each little one full throttle - not by fits and starts or according to how well they behave.

Lord, help me become such an effective witness to Divine Love that my children will never question that their births were cosmic events as are the births of every other human being, and that, nipped in the bud, we'll miss their blooming. Help me, Lord, to respect each and every little one as you do - full throttle. And let my children grow up feeling that love to their very core. Holy Spirit, I entrust my fatherhood to You.

IV

THE PRESENTATION

"They took him up to Jerusalem to present him to the Lord."

Luke 2:22

In the West, we call this event the presentation of Christ in the temple. In the East they call it "the meeting." Both titles are correct, and are the same story but from a different perspective - like looking at a building from two sides.

The presentation and formal meeting most of us fathers have with our children is that initial glance provided by the labor and delivery nurse. It is a brief first meeting, because nurses tend to then rush off to clean the baby up. But, when she returns that blanket-swaddled bundle to our arms, we gaze into that baby's eyes and pour out our hearts, if not in words, then in speechless exhilaration like no other language spoken in any other facet of our lives. This meeting starts a "conversation" with our children that continues into eternity. It mirrors another eternal conversation our children will engage in - the one that begins when they are baptized.

The communication between God and his first children, Adam and Eve, was broken off, not by God, but by His children. Jesus came to renew the conversation between God the Father and His people, giving us, among the seven Sacraments, the great gift of Baptism. The waters of Baptism wash clean the stain of original sin, allowing our children to take up that conversation with God, first through their mom and dad, and eventually, as they grow older, for themselves. Our job as fathers is to see, all through their formation at home, that the conversation with God is kept active, respectful and full of trust.

Meeting someone does not insure there will ever be a conversation. It may remain just a meeting with no words exchanged, no meaning conveyed, nothing of ourselves shared with the other. Event over. How sad it would be if our encounter with God remained only a meeting, or if we failed to do our best to provide an environment where our children can hear the voice of God and respond to Him in awe and adoration.

Dear Lord, help me keep the conversation with You and with my children going, so they might understand what it is to be fully attentive to the voice of the beloved. May my entire household be in daily conversation with You. Holy Spirit, I entrust my fatherhood to You.

V

FINDING JESUS IN THE TEMPLE

"When his parents saw him, they were astonished, and his mother said to him, "Son, why have you done this to us? Your father and I have been looking for you with great anxiety." And he said to them, "Why were you looking for me? Did you not know that I must be in my Father's House?"

Luke 2:48-49

Jesus loved to be in His Father's "house," and that is where Our Lady found him. The fear that must have gripped Mary upon losing Jesus was, no doubt, quickly replaced by the joy of realizing that her boy wanted to stay in "Church" and take part in it.

When my wife and I were raising the children, and we were attending a Byzantine Catholic parish that offered donuts after the Divine Liturgy, our little ones *loved* to go! They called it "the church with the donuts." An adult response to that would be that they should rather be happy because they are going there for God - not donuts. But you cannot put an old head on young shoulders. Right understanding comes in an age-appropriate package. Our children's joy of attending Mass (even if for a less noble

reason) opened their hearts to the formation of good memories about church, good associations with the other children there, and all kinds of benefits. In time, they were singing parts of the Liturgy in Old Slavonic! They had absolutely no idea what they were singing, but they were there, participating. The donuts became something we got to have after we did what we do in the Church. The idea of duty and obligation come later. Parents teach their children. The Holy Spirit calls their hearts. And a life-long habit of being found in their Father's house gets established. They might leave that habit when they are on their own, but the Lord knows how and when to call them back – in the manner that He knows is best. Good memories can make them long to return. That's what we as parents are helping to build now – the understanding that something special is in store for them when they walk through the doors of their church, something unlike anything else out in the world. The conversation between God and our children is a lot more productive when they look forward to the time they spend with Him.

Dear God, help me be joyful in my faith and happy to take my family to Mass. Let my face show it! Holy Spirit, I entrust my fatherhood to You.

THE LUMINOUS MYSTERIES

I

THE BAPTISM OF JESUS

"After Jesus was baptized, he came up from the water and behold, the heavens were opened for him, and he saw the Spirit of God descending like a dove and coming upon him."

Matthew 3:16

I remember how excited we were to baptize our children! How different each one was. How unique. We couldn't help but see the truth of St. Therese's comment about souls being as different as faces. Zellie Martin, the mother of St. Therese, knew she had to form each daughter's soul according to its own character.

In my pastoral work, I have witnessed different stages in the spiritual life. In the sacred agenda of the Holy Spirit, virtually everything is custom designed to work with each soul. His design is not "one size fits all". The rigorous lessons that will inspire one little soul will prove just too daunting for another. Wisdom, wisdom, wisdom! That is my daily prayer! A great theologian has said three doors stand before souls, each of them leading to God. One is Truth, one is Holiness, and a third is Beauty.

One soul is drawn by one or the other, or different ones at different times.

Mary is Beauty! She can draw my soul when I don't feel holy or when the truth is giving me an argument. She comes to me and just loves me. Truth and Holiness come with her, but don't speak about themselves because at that particular time I will not be able to listen.

Dear Jesus, you call each of your lambs "by name". You know what each one needs and at what time in their lives they need it. Help me know my children's souls so well that I can help provide them what they need for their journey with you. Holy Spirit, I entrust my fatherhood to You.

II

THE WEDDING FEAST AT CANA

"When the wine ran short, the mother of Jesus said to him, 'They have no wine.' And Jesus said to her, 'Woman, how does your concern affect me? My hour has not yet come.' His mother said to the servers, 'Do whatever he tells you.'"

John 2:3-5

In this mystery, Jesus works his first miracle, and the disciples begin to believe in him. The exchange between Jesus and his mother provides such a telling look into their family life! Mary was once again attending to the needs of a relative (likely a very close relative), and involves Jesus immediately.

Mary is the perfect model for us. We need to immediately involve Jesus in all our affairs, especially those of our family members, and not just turn to Him as a last resort.

But Jesus doesn't always respond immediately and often not in the timely manner *we* think He should. He wants to see faith in some cases, or the time is not right, or He wants to provide an important lesson. In any case, at the wedding feast, Mary doesn't hesitate to assume He *will* act.

Of course He will! So she tells the servants to do whatever He tells them to do. And they show their faith by doing it, no questions asked. So much of my prayer is without faith and I often fail to realize that the way He answers has to be the wise way - His way. And His way will always be informed by divine love. Wisdom informed by love.

Mary is our intercessor with Jesus, just as she was for the family giving the wedding feast. His answer was wise and full of love - and became known by many more than those who were there. One of the saints I like to read advises we go to Mary, present our need, ask her to tell Jesus - and then trust that there will be an answer. Not the answer we dictate! We are not the ones with the wisdom! Our love doesn't reach out to consider our enemy most of the time. If we fail so miserably, at times, to see the wisdom in God withholding what we want and sometimes giving us what we don't ask for, you know our children will fail to see it as well. None of us wants to suffer. But sometimes, it is necessary for our own good or someone else's.

One of my children found out his mother and I had a regular prayer we added to our Rosary petitions when we prayed it together. "Dear God, if our children are into something that will hurt them, please let them get caught the first time." He came to me and said, "Dad - stop praying that!" He had a big smile on his face, but it was obvious he had been caught at something that wasn't going to be good for him, and he knew it. He didn't want to suffer the consequence, even though, in the end, it would save him.

Dear Lord, help me set aside my poor wisdom and faulty love so I can trust you will answer in your perfect wisdom and immeasurable love when Mary comes to you with my request. Holy Spirit, I entrust my fatherhood to You.

III

THE PROCLAMATION OF THE KINGDOM

"After John had been arrested, Jesus came to Galilee proclaiming the gospel of God: 'This is the time of fulfillment. The kingdom of God is at hand. Repent, and believe in the gospel.'"

Mark 1:14-15

Jesus travelled from village to town, teaching what is needed for us to live in the Kingdom – beginning here and opening fully in Heaven. Don't let anger loose on anyone. Forgive. Love your enemies. Don't judge. These are like laws in the Kingdom of God. How on earth can we do all of that? Jesus gives us the answer: become like little children. "Learn from me, for I am gentle and humble of heart."

Giving intellectual assent to these things is one thing – living them from day to day in front of my family and God is quite another. Anyone who hears these teachings and doesn't follow them is like someone who stares into a mirror, but forgets what he looks like the minute he stops looking.

One morning, I was just about ready to process down the aisle for the 10:45 Mass, when I realized I better get a drink of water

because my voice was so husky. As I approached the drinking fountain, a kid, maybe seven or eight, reached it at the same time. Of course the thought came that I had a mission, and I'm the priest, and it is time to start the Mass and the boy can drink after me. As I put out my hand to stop him and walked forward, the Lord stopped me in my tracks. It wasn't a voice, but I understood immediately that I was to invite the boy to go first. Mass would wait. As I watched the boy drink, I understood something I had ignored before – in the Kingdom of God, the last are first. "Let the little children come to me," Jesus told the disciples. The Kingdom of God is made up of such as these.

Pauline Martin, St. Therese's older sister, taught that lessons God teaches us specifically and individually are so important that we must use them as precious guides in our spiritual life. Love of God and neighbor is one side of the coin. Humility before God and neighbor is the other side. Like a double strand stringing pearls together, love and humility keep virtues from getting away! For us men, who often receive worldly rewards for fighting until we get our way, it's not always easy to be humble. But as fathers, we must strive to model humility and love for our children, so they might begin to string their own double strand of virtues and receive the true and eternal reward – that of pleasing Jesus.

Lord, help me remember that day at the fountain, and always stay very small so I can fit in your Kingdom. And may I help my children see the beauty in remaining small as well. Holy Spirit, I entrust my fatherhood to You.

IV

THE TRANSFIGURATION

"Lord, it is good that we are here."
Mark 17:4

I love rocks - all kinds of rocks. When I was little, I carried pockets full of rocks home. Especially, I love polished gem stones. I think a lot of life-lessons can be learned from the great beauty God has displayed in nature, and in our using His creation to create more beauty. After all, we are His image!

Of all the rocks I have collected, I am particularly fond of a plain, gray, totally uninteresting lump that looks like anything you would dig up. But once broken open, it exposes glorious amethyst formations. I have it right in front of Our Lady of Guadalupe in my prayer corner because I know she loves beautiful gem stones. Tepeyac was covered with them. The Indian writer who describes the vegetation of that hill where she appeared in 1500s Mexico speaks of this. In the Revelation of St. John the Divine, heaven and Jesus' throne are described in these terms as well. So, while not a profound theologically deep insight, I believe rocks reflect the beauty of God as all of nature does, and I know He loves absolutely everything He has made. When I look at that plain rock, hiding the dazzling Amethyst, I can imagine the transfiguration. The Church Fathers say Jesus wears Humility like a garment - lowly and not extraordinary. He wore His humanity in the same way, veiling His Divinity. In the Transfiguration, Jesus was "broken open" for that moment in time to reveal the beauty of His Divinity.

As fathers, we must remember that our children are also like that favorite rock of mine. They hold within them the potential to be taken to the right hand of the Triune Divinity to stand beside Jesus forever, sharing intimacy with God. Jesus is there by nature. My children can be there as sons and daughters of God by Grace. But for that, humility is required. It is the humble that God draws near, and the arrogant that He resists!

Dear Lord, help me clothe myself with humility as God does, in all of my dealings with my family. And teach them to clothe themselves in the same way, that something glorious might grow within them. Holy Spirit, I entrust my fatherhood to You.

V

THE INSTITUTION OF THE HOLY EUCHARIST

"Jesus took bread, said the blessing, broke it and giving it to his disciples said, 'Take and eat. This is my body.' Then he took a cup, gave thanks and gave it to them, saying, 'drink from it, all of you, for this is my blood of the Covenant, which will be shed on behalf of many for the forgiveness of sins.'"

Matthew 26:26-27

I spent some time as pastor of a little Byzantine Catholic Church. After the Liturgy, people would come forward for a blessing and to kiss the cross I held. A neighborhood girl of eight or nine attended regularly. She would just walk in and join us for many Sundays. One day she brought me a picture she had drawn and colored. It was a lamb, a cup, and a cross. She had written beneath it these words: EAT THE BREAD AND KISS THE CROSS! I did not sit her down and explain why the Divine Liturgy is much more than that. We need always remember that children learn things best when the material is age appropriate. We start our children on a simple diet and in time, we feed them richer fare, so that their understanding develops in a natural way.

When Jesus instituted the Eucharist, He gave us Bread from Heaven for our journey to the Kingdom - our Promised Land. It is our daily bread. If we ourselves love the Eucharist and see it as nourishment we cannot live without, our children will become aware of their constant need for this Bread of Life - even more than their need of a daily vitamin! We don't take our children to the Holy Sacrifice of the Mass because it is a mortal sin if we don't and God will shake His finger at them. We teach them that this is our Holy Food in this life and instill in them gratitude and understanding of how fortunate we are that Jesus loved us enough to provide it.

When I think about this Mystery, I have to think of the many things that the Passover and the Sacrifice of the Mass have in common. Both deal with leaving slavery and journeying toward a promised land, both have a sacrifice, both a "meal," and both are commanded memorials: "Do this in memory of me." As well, both speak of manna from Heaven. I became fascinated with all of this when I read Brant Pitre's *Jesus and the Jewish Roots of the Eucharist*. I had to marvel at the unfathomable wisdom and creativity of the Lord of History. And yet, despite all the intellectual and theological explanations we can give our children, perhaps none is as powerful as witnessing the glow on my face when I receive our Lord in Holy Communion.

Jesus, help me to always show my children the wonder and beauty of our Faith – and let them see my love and reverence for your sacred Body and Blood, especially when I don't even know they are watching. Holy Spirit, I entrust my fatherhood to You.

THE SORROWFUL MYSTERIES

I

AGONY IN THE GARDEN

"Not my will, but yours be done."
Luke 22:42

We face many deaths in life. Some are of our own making - like losing a job because we didn't give it our best. But in our journey to the fullness of the Kingdom of God, nothing is there just by accident. If we believe in the providence of God, we can be called to abandon ourselves to it. That means we take every day's events as being there because God willed them or didn't step in to stop them. We can say, "It is what it is - now Lord, show me how to deal with it." St. Therese said she had no peace in her soul until she started her day with that orientation. Then, trusting God to walk beside her, she finished her journey as the woman four popes called the greatest saint of modern times.

In my family there have been many "deaths" to navigate. The deaths expected in the spiritual life account for most of them. The death of pride, the death of greed, the death of selfishness, the death of anger, the death of one vice after another. Each of these deaths hurts, but each also brings the joy of new life in Christ! A very little "death" can break open a wonderful gift.

Driving on the Hollywood Freeway as we went from Universal Studios back to our hotel in LA, I felt the nudge to pray the Rosary with my family. We kept a basket of plastic rosaries between the seats for just such nudges. At home, the children never complained, but we were on vacation! "Oh, Dad, do we have to?" Half way through the decades, with traffic whizzing along at 80 mph or more, a car passed us on the right - upside down! Groceries were rolling out the open windows - oranges, paper towels. We all gasped. It slowed down thanks to friction, and we looked back to see traffic stopped. Realizing how close it had come to hitting us, one of the kids said, "Wow, Dad!" - and no one complained that we finished our prayer. Such events, provided really by Providence, teach much more than words.

Lord, help me depend on your help when I am wanting to bring my children along in their faith. Help me show that little sacrifices can do great things. Holy Spirit, I entrust my fatherhood to You.

II

THE SCOURGING AT THE PILLAR

"By His stripes we were healed."
Isaiah 53:5

Some years ago, I buried a young girl who died from an inoperable brain tumor. She suffered it bravely, but it was like a scourging and hard to watch. Her Grandmother was raising her because her mom had died – I think of an overdose. The Grandmother had kept her daughter's ashes at home, not yet ready to part with them.

I remember very well the day the little girl died. The sky was as dark as coal, it was pouring down rain, and there was – all morning – no break in the darkness. I went to the Grandmother's home and anointed the girl. One of my daughters went with me – she was just entering her teen years. I wanted her to see and be compassionate. She did, and she was!

When the girl's breaths were getting farther and farther apart, they finally just stopped – and the sun literally exploded through that bedroom window and my daughter said, "Look Dad, a rainbow!" It was true. Out of all that blackness came the light, and with it a beautiful rainbow that filled the sky. The grandmother put her daughter's ashes in the little girl's casket, and they were buried together. I firmly believe that children who suffer a scourging, a deadly illness or abuse or war or any other "cruelty," are met by Jesus when they enter heaven, and He gives them nickels to spend any way they like. I believe this little girl spent her first one on her mother, for some great blessing! We call it "an exchange of spiritual goods," which is all nice and theologically tidy, but in reality it is wrapped in a great love - on our part and on God's part.

Jesus, help me teach my children that what appears so dark and foreboding can be filled with something infinitely good. Holy Spirit, I entrust my fatherhood to You.

III

THE CROWNING WITH THORNS

"Weaving a crown of thorns, they placed it on his head and a reed in his right hand. And kneeling before him, they mocked Him, saying, 'Hail, King of the Jews!' They spat upon Him..."

Matthew 27:29-30

In this mystery Jesus is mocked for calling himself the King of the Jews. He is being bullied - cruelly and painfully. The sad thing is not only that Jesus is being tormented, but that the tormentors are being dehumanized by their own cruelty. God created us in His own image, and since his defining core is love, so is ours. How far bullying is from who and what we are!

Not all bullying is physical, but all of it is painful. On one of my trips to a mountainous shrine, people were climbing a high and very steep hill. My fourteen-year-old son was with me. A large group of pilgrims from Haiti arrived, and headed up the hill. It was very hot that day - the sun was relentless. One of the women was very heavy, and was trying to go up the hill in shoes that did not support her at all. She sat on a rock, all alone, and tried to regain her strength. Someone commented that

someone her size shouldn't be trying to climb the hill to the holy site. It sounded like mocking to me. I don't know if my son heard that comment or not. He said to me, "Dad, look at that woman over there. She's hot and doesn't have any water. Can I give her some of mine?" I was so proud of him in that moment. He went over to her and gave her his water. It was all so natural to him. The image of God was manifest in that event, much more powerfully than any lesson I could have planned. For me, it was the highlight of the whole pilgrimage.

Jesus, let the light of love shine from my children as a witness to who they really are. Help me keep teaching them about their dignity in creation. Holy Spirit, I entrust my fatherhood to You.

IV

THE CARRYING OF THE CROSS

"As they were going out, they met a Cyrenian named Simon; this man they pressed into service to carry the cross."

Matthew 27:32

Just as so many beautiful things are hidden in what appears to be the blackest moments in life, resurrection is already present in death. Jesus made that possible. When we think of His life, we can see that his dying began already in His birth. Just as it is for all of us, death was written in – but so was the Father's plan for Jesus' glorious triumph. Someone once said we need to get our dying over with, so that our eternal life becomes our focus.

Many years ago, a woman I knew was suffering from calcium problems and her spine was deteriorating, as well as other bones. Confined to home, she worked daily on her soul. Patience, love and gentleness grew in the confines of the prison cell her body was fast becoming. Finally, so worn out, she entered the hospital for yet another round of tests and treatments. Then I got the call: "Father, can you come to see me right away!"

Of course I went, and found her full of joy. I asked her what the doctor was telling her, thinking it must be what put the radiance on her face. She said they told her that, apart from her bones, she was healthy and would be able to go home in two days. But, she said,

Jesus had stood in the doorway of her room the night before and raised His hands in a gesture of welcome. He smiled and told her He was taking her home to heaven.

As the woman was telling me this, her husband entered the room and asked me to talk some sense into her. The doctors had given her a clean bill of health, he confirmed, apart from her bones, and there was no reason for her to think she was going to die. It was, of course, useless to try to convince her. She had seen Jesus.

The next morning I went back to the hospital to see her again, and a nun was just coming out. The woman had died in her sleep overnight -- such a shock, the nun said.

It wasn't a shock to the woman. Jesus had prepared her for the journey, not just by His recent visit, but by walking with her on her way of suffering. She had taken up her cross years earlier, and used it to sanctify her soul. Her resurrection was written right into all that suffering. And so it can be for us as well, if we recognize everything - even our trials -- as a necessary part of our journey toward heaven. So much easier said than done. But critical for us as fathers to show our children that we trust God so much, we can rejoice in our suffering, knowing He permits it because He loves us beyond all measure and will use it for our salvation.

Lord, help me show my children, by the patient endurance of my own crosses, that suffering can be transformed into something of great value. Holy Spirit, I entrust my fatherhood to you.

V

THE CRUCIFIXION

" The earth quaked, rocks were split, tombs were opened and the bodies of many saints who had fallen asleep were raised."

Matthew 27:51-52

When we look at Jesus on the cross, we cannot help but see his perfect love for us. We make a great deal of the fact that Jesus loved us, *unto the end*. So much of the love we see in our world does not endure unto the end. In fact, many popular songs lament this. The divorce rate is now over fifty percent, despite the Church's teaching that God intends for marriage to be permanent.

In my experience, it is love that makes the difference. Love will endure when everything else falls apart. A marriage that has authentic love can triumph when other marriages crash. Marriage requires the kind of love that Jesus has for us. Perhaps that is why St. Paul compares the Sacrament of Marriage with the relationship of Christ and His Church – His people.

A beautiful Eastern icon of Jesus, scourged and holding his scepter of reed, is titled *Extreme Humility*. But its other title is *The Bridegroom*. Jesus is so intent on helping us understand that love is the defining core of God, that He makes it our fundamental vocation. Love that endures unto the end is the kind of love we as husbands and fathers are called to. It is the kind of love families must strive to foster because it is a very reflection of God Himself.

The Catechism of the Catholic Church specifically tells us that love is the fundamental vocation of every baptized person. That means my vocation of Priesthood is secondary to my vocation to love - and that is true of virtually every vocation that exists. Faith, hope and love abide - but the greatest of these is love. Faith will be unnecessary one day. What we believed in will be realized right in front of us. Hope will end, because all we hoped for will be fulfilled. But love alone endures on the other side of death - and it endures forever.

How must we, as husbands and fathers, love those God has entrusted to us? If we are to be a mirror of God's love, we must love unconditionally. Unto the end. My children will never be perfect in this life. But Jesus, while we were yet sinners, died for us. The parable of the Good Samaritan is a perfect icon of Jesus' love, which tends and heals those beaten up by this world. The father in the parable of the

Prodigal Son is an exact icon of God the Father. His love stands and waits for the return of the child who has abandoned all goodness in his futile search for something better. It waits in hope that, one day, the boy will realize there is nothing better than the embrace of unconditional, unending love.

Lord, help me reflect Divine love in all of my daily actions. Help me always to do what love requires - just as you do. Help me love unto the end. Holy Spirit, I entrust my fatherhood to You.

THE GLORIOUS MYSTERIES

I

THE RESURRECTION

"Do not let your hearts be troubled ... In my father's house there are many dwelling places. If there were not, would I have told you that I am going to prepare a place for you? And if I go and prepare a place for you, I will come back again and take you to myself, so that where I am you also may be."

John 14: 1-3

Just about every time a child loses a pet, there is that question - is Fluffy in heaven? My answer is always the same - with God, nothing is impossible! That answer always points to faith in God and in His love for everything He has made. Just about any other answer clamps a limit on God and confines Him to a kind of dogmatic prison.

We know that we humans are the ones God gifted with an immortal soul and therefore the promise of the possibility of sharing in the life of the Holy Trinity, in complete union with Him. Only we are made in His image. But when God speaks of the Kingdom as a new heaven and a new earth, does that erase everything that wasn't immortal to start with? If God wants Fluffy in Paradise, I can tell you, that little ball of fuzz will be there!

The resurrection of Jesus from the dead is the essential piece in our own hope of eternal life. As Paul teaches, if Christ is not risen, our own hope is in vain. Jesus raised Lazarus as a glorious sign of our own resurrection. He *is* the resurrection and the life!

When my little brother died at age five in the polio epidemic of the 1940's, his body lay in state in our house until the funeral the next day. When the hearse drove him away, my grandfather told me that was the last time I would see him until heaven. I was only nine, but his faith supported my own. I knew I would see him again someday.

Jesus, fill me with strong faith and joyful hope, so my children will always remember my witness to the resurrection. Help us live our lives with our eyes fixed on heaven, where we will live in union with You in perfect love. Holy Spirit, I entrust my fatherhood to You.

II

THE ASCENSION

"As he blessed them, he parted from them and was taken up to heaven."

Luke 24:51

For Jesus, the ascension is a return home. He existed before his conception in the womb of Mary. As for the rest of us, our souls did not exist before we were conceived. But our theology does indeed teach that God knows us by name and, as St. Therese would say, "loves us unto madness" long before we come into existence.

If I really understand that God has loved each of my kids long before I ever dreamed of having them, I also have to figure He has a specific hope for them. The Church explains that Divine hope very simply. God wants us to come to know Him, to come to love Him, to serve Him in some way in this life, and to come to His embrace in Heaven when we die. In this way, we do indeed return home, because we have always existed in that furnace of love that is the heart of God.

It is our duty and our joy, as parents, to convey this Divine hope to our children. Parents are the first and primary teachers of their children. We hold that honor as a gift from God. While the Church will give plenty of help, especially in preparing our children for Sacraments, life itself also offers invaluable teachable moments. A relative dies, and we gather the kids and talk about what that person meant to each of us. Then we kneel and ask God to welcome our loved one home. Such moments provide our children with memories that validate our core beliefs. Our children see our faith put into practice and come to practice it as their own.

Jesus, help us model family prayer while our children are young. Help us give them prayer experiences that are rich in shared faith and laden with the Divine hope of the eternal embrace. Holy Spirit, I entrust my fatherhood to You.

III

THE DESCENT OF THE HOLY SPIRIT

"If you love me, you will keep my commandments. And I will ask the Father, and He will give you another advocate to be with you always, the Spirit of truth, which the world cannot accept, because it neither sees nor knows it. But you know it, because it remains with you, and will be in you. I will not leave you orphans; I will come to you."

John 14:15-17

One day I was sitting in a corner of an atrium - a classroom used for the Catechesis of the Good Shepherd, where children come to learn about the Faith. As the teacher and I watched the children with their various works, I saw a child of seven put his hands over a small chalice, using the gesture a priest uses to ask that the Holy Spirit descend over the wine and change it into the blood of Christ. The child was imitating an epiclesis, just as he'd seen his priest do many times in various sacraments and in the blessing of sacramentals. I got to thinking about using this sacred gesture to call the Holy Spirit to descend on families and their homes. Mom can use it, Dad, kids, anyone.

The descent of the Holy Spirit at Pentecost empowered the Church to do its great work. The family is called the "domestic church." It, too, has great work to do. Faithfulness on the part of parents, mutual love and respect, order and loving obedience on the part of children, little sacrifices on everyone's part - these are important ingredients in family life.

The domestic church must be a school of love - for God and for neighbor. What a great act of love it would be if we would encourage our whole family to extend their hands over a sick one, or over school work that needs the Holy Spirit's inspiration, or even over a clogged drain or a house cat who refuses to keep its claws off the curtains! Teaching children to depend on the help of the Holy Spirit chips away at the temptation to think they are their own higher power. Teaching them to accept the Holy Spirit's providence teaches them humility and gratitude.

Jesus, you sent the Holy Spirit to be our helper and guide on our way to your Kingdom. Help me trust and depend on His wisdom and teach my children to do the same. Holy Spirit, I entrust my fatherhood to You.

IV

THE ASSUMPTION

"Therefore my heart is glad and my soul rejoices, my body, too, abides in confidence; Because you will not abandon my soul to the nether world, nor will you suffer your faithful one to undergo corruption."

Psalms 16:9-10

You could use so many theological truths to explain the Assumption of Mary. She shared in Jesus' passion. She is sinless. As mother of God, she has her work as the new Eve. And there are more. But one overrides all others in the hearts of the faithful: She's our Mother! We need her beside Jesus – body and soul in heaven. We need to see her already living and working as Our Mother and as Mother of the Church.

Once, when I was not yet Catholic, I asked the Holy Spirit to tell me what Mary's work is. The answer came in a half-asleep "dream." I saw a great mansion covering an entire city block. There were kids on the sidewalk by the kitchen entrance. They looked like homeless kids right out of a Charles Dickens story. Suddenly the door opened and a woman I assumed was Mary gathered them all inside. She cleaned them up, sat them at the table and taught them how to behave in the refined life of the mansion. They could not, for example, steal the silverware! She was doing this all and entirely for the Lord of the mansion. After a great deal of work, over time, each was ready to walk up the big staircase to the great room to meet the Master of the house, who welcomed them as his very own.

Eve fed us poison. Mary feeds us bread from heaven. She takes us in and mothers our souls in the way her spouse, the Holy Spirit, teaches her. I never want to forget how she cared for those children in my "dream." As a father, it gives me great comfort to know she will take care of my family in the same way.

Jesus, help me model love for our Mother so my children will love her and allow her to form them. Holy Spirit, I entrust my fatherhood to You.

V

THE CORONATION

"A great sign appeared in the sky, a woman clothed with the sun, with the moon under her feet, and on her head a crown of twelve stars."

Revelations 12:1

"Hail Holy Queen!" We all know that prayer. Yet, our Little Flower, St. Therese, says, "Oh, she is much more mother than queen!" As a dad, I'm the male head of my family line. My wife is the female head. Patriarch and matriarch. And yet, to follow Christ's model, I need to be much more father than patriarch. I need to be much more he who is loved, and therefore obeyed, than he who is king and therefore must be feared.

The balance between authority and loving respect is not always easy for fathers to achieve. But if Jesus corrected His disciples for wanting to be in places of authority - at his right hand or his left in His kingdom - we dads need to figure out what the combined roles of father and servant look like. Of course, our wives will say you can wash dishes and still be a real man. Well, therein lies a clue. Real men serve.

If we keep the ideal of the Holy Family ever before us - the ideal of mutual love and respect -- we won't over-extend our authority and forget our place as servant.

What makes Mary such a beautiful queen is she never sought the seat of royalty. She sought only to serve: "I am the Handmaid of the Lord." How pleased Jesus must have been to bestow Heaven's choicest crown on Mary, who never sought to wear a crown, only a veil of perfect humility.

May the Blessed Mother form my soul in humility as well, so my children will follow in my ways as her children have followed in hers – drawn by the power of perfect love. Holy Spirit, I entrust my fatherhood to you.

HOW TO PRAY THE ROSARY

1. While holding the crucifix, make the SIGN OF THE CROSS: "In the name of the Father, and of the Son and of the Holy Spirit. Amen."

2. Then, recite the APOSTLE'S CREED:
"I BELIEVE IN GOD, the Father almighty, Creator of heaven and earth, and in Jesus Christ, his only Son, our Lord, who was conceived by the Holy Spirit, born of the Virgin Mary, suffered under Pontius Pilate, was crucified, died and was buried; he descended into hell; on the third day he rose again from the dead; he ascended into heaven, and is seated at the right hand of God the Father almighty; from there he will come to judge the living and the dead. I believe in the Holy Spirit, the holy catholic Church, the communion of saints, the forgiveness of sins, the resurrection of the body, and life everlasting. Amen."

3. Recite the OUR FATHER on the first large Bead:
"OUR FATHER, Who art in heaven, Hallowed be Thy Name. Thy Kingdom come. Thy Will be done, on earth as it is in Heaven. Give us this day our daily bread. And forgive us our trespasses, as we forgive those who trespass against us. And lead us

not into temptation, but deliver us from evil. Amen."

4. On each of the three small beads, recite a HAIL MARY for the increase of faith, hope and love. "HAIL MARY, full of grace, the Lord is with thee; Blessed art thou among women, and blessed is the fruit of thy womb, Jesus. Holy Mary, Mother of God, pray for us sinners, now and at the hour of death. Amen."

5. Recite the GLORY BE on the next large bead.
"GLORY BE to the Father, and to the Son, and to the Holy Spirit. As it was in the beginning, is now, and ever shall be, world without end. Amen."

6. Recall the first Rosary Mystery and recite the Our Father on the next large bead.

7. On each of the adjacent ten small beads (known as a decade), recite a Hail Mary while reflecting on the mystery.

8. On the next large bead, recite the Glory Be.

9. The FATIMA PRAYER may be said here:
"O MY JESUS, forgive us our sins, save us from the fires of hell, lead all souls to

heaven, especially those who are in most need of Thy mercy."

10. Begin the next decade by recalling the next mystery and reciting an Our Father. Move to the small beads and pray 10 Hail Marys while meditating on the mystery.

11. Continue until you have circled the entire
Rosary (five decades.) Or for a full Rosary, you will circle it four times (twenty decades.)

12. It is customary to CONCLUDE with the following prayers:

HAIL HOLY QUEEN

"HAIL, HOLY QUEEN, mother of mercy, our life, our sweetness, and our hope. To thee do we cry, poor banished children of Eve. To thee do we send up our sighs, mourning and weeping in this valley of tears. Turn then, most gracious advocate, thine eyes of mercy toward us, and after this our exile, show us the blessed fruit of thy womb, Jesus. O clement, O loving, O sweet Virgin Mary.
(Verse) Pray for us, O Holy Mother of God.
(Response) That we may be made worthy of the promises of Christ."

ROSARY PRAYER

(Verse) Let us pray,
(Response) O God, whose only begotten Son, by His life, death, and resurrection, has purchased for us the rewards of eternal salvation, grant, we beseech Thee, that while meditating on these mysteries of the most holy Rosary of the Blessed Virgin Mary, that we may both imitate what they contain and obtain what they promise, through Christ our Lord. Amen.

Most Sacred Heart of Jesus, have mercy on us.

Immaculate Heart of Mary, pray for us.

In the Name of the Father, and of the Son and of the Holy Spirit. Amen.

FICTION AVAILABLE FROM
Caritas Press / Catholic Word

Until Lily

Wherever Lily Goes

Life Entwined with Lily's

Sherry Boas' life-changing series that has been called: **"masterful," "profound," "riveting," "heart-wrenching"** and **"made for our times."**

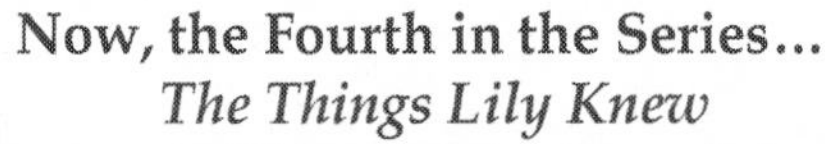

Now, the Fourth in the Series...
The Things Lily Knew

A brilliant Rhodes Scholar whose love life is torn in threes, Annabel Greeley is not lacking in wit or intellect. But when the accomplished geneticist is faced with a decision that will change, not only her life, but the future of humanity, the answers elude her. She is hounded by the ever-present and unavoidable fact that she would not be alive if it weren't for her Aunt Lily, who happened to have Down syndrome and, seemingly, all of life's answers. Annabel's life is about to change in profound and paradoxical ways as she sets out in search of the things Lily knew.

Visit www.LilyTrilogy.com

www.LilyTrilogy.com

Caritas Press

(602) 920-2846

Sherry@LilyTrilogy.com

Made in the USA
Middletown, DE
04 December 2015